HOW TO DEVELOP
A BETTER
SELF-IMAGE

Russell M. Abata, C.SS.R., S.T.D.

LIGUORI
PUBLICATIONS

One Liguori Drive
Liguori, Missouri 63057
(314) 464-2500

Imprimi Potest:
Edmund T. Langton, C.SS.R.
Provincial, St. Louis Province
Redemptorist Fathers

Imprimatur:
+ John N. Wurm, S.T.D., Ph.D.
Vicar General, Archdiocese of St. Louis

Copyright © 1980, Liguori Publications
ISBN 0-89243-119-9
Library of Congress Catalog Card Number: 79-91440

Printed in U.S.A.

Photo by David Muench
from the H. Armstrong Roberts Studio

*This book is dedicated to
those people who are
courageous enough to ask
the all-important question:
WHO AM I? WHO AM I, REALLY?*

TABLE OF CONTENTS

Introduction 7

1. Setting the Stage 9

2. Training —
   Painting by the Numbers 13

3. Feelings — A One-sided Portrait 31

4. A Full-length Picture 43

5. Accepting All of You 59

6. Too Much "I" 67

7. Your Real Personality and Others 71

8. When the Other Is God 85

Conclusion 95

INTRODUCTION

Ask yourself a serious question.

Do you ever hit periods when everything seems unsure and you wonder what you, God, and life are all about?

Things might be going along smoothly. It is not that you do not have problems. There are problems, but somehow you can manage them. But then a problem comes along that you do not feel you can handle. You cannot ignore it or run away from it. What are you to do? You are not sure. All you know is that a landslide is taking place inside of you, and you are trying to hold on to whatever security you have, like a wind-beaten oak tree holding on to the ground by the fingers of its roots.

You turn to God and it seems that he has stopped listening to your prayers. You turn to a special friend and that only helps a little. You do not know what to do. All you know is that you feel bad and cannot shake the feeling.

Where is this bad feeling coming from? Is it a punishment? Is it a temptation from an evil source? Is it just a part of some bad luck you are experiencing?

Most likely such down feelings are the results of too many pressures. You are trying to do too much or you are approaching your problems the wrong way. Your feelings are working against you, not for you. They need to be straightened out. Hopefully this book can help you to straighten them out.

God has made you most special. Your main task in life is to find and develop that special you. This will give God the glory he deserves for making such a wonderful creation, and it will give you the maximum happiness you are capable of, both in this life and in eternal life.

But there are complications in trying to discover and develop this special you. It is so easy to confuse what others want you to be or what your feelings want you to be with the special person God wants you to be. In this book we will try to help you sort out who you really are, so that you, God, and others can help you develop it.

Questions

1. Can you describe how you felt when you were down?
2. Was there anyone with whom you could talk out your feelings?
3. Did you pray more at that time or did you feel that God did not care about how you felt?
4. Did your bad feelings go away on their own or did you have to do something to get rid of them?
5. Did those bad feelings make you wonder whether there was something wrong with you?

1
SETTING
THE
STAGE

Of all the powers God has given you to help you to cope with life and to discover him as the author of life, your feelings rank high in importance.

Although it is your power of reason that makes you human and different from animals, it is how you feel that most often determines how you will function. In some ways your feelings are more important to you than the blood that helps sustain your life. Your feelings add a new dimension of life to your physical life.

But despite their importance, your feelings can present you with some very serious difficulties.

There are times when you will cherish your feelings as your greatest treasure. There are times when you might wish you had been born without feelings.

Today your feelings can make you so strong that you feel you could stand up to the world. Tomorrow they can make you feel so scared and weak that all you want to do is cry or hide somewhere.

There are times when your feelings will have you praise God for the life he has given you. At other times they can have you resent God for giving you life.

Supported by deep, positive feelings, you can become a hero or saint. Driven by intense, negative feelings, you can destroy whatever you touch.

So your feelings are a tremendous potential for good or bad. It depends on how they are supervised. The Bible recognized this a long time ago when it warned, "With closest custody, guard your heart, for in it are the sources of life" (Proverbs 4:23).

Two Candidates

Looking into your personality, we find two forces that are capable of supervising your feelings.

One force is your training.

The other force is your real personality.

How do the two differ?

Your training is a way of acting imposed on you from the outside. Your parents, teachers, and other "big" people have told you how to act and how not to act. If they were really thorough, they might even have told you what to feel and what not to feel.

For convenience we refer to their directives as the "dos" and "don'ts" of your training.

Your real personality is not something that comes from the outside. It is a force that comes from you. It is a wonder inside of you, and in each of us, so tremendous that you would think that God got the idea for each of us by taking a multibillion number of snapshots of himself and creating us according to those miniature pictures of himself. We have some confirmation of this from the Scriptures when it says, "God created man in his image; in the divine image he created him; male and female he created them" (Genesis 1:27).

We will see a great deal more of your real personality later in this book.

These, then, your training and your real personality, are the two available candidates for supervising your feelings.

The Better Supervisor

Which of these two candidates — your training or the personality from your own being — is the better supervisor of your feelings?

This really is not a good question. Depending on the time and condition of your life, both have their rightful place in directing your life.

When you were young, your training was about the only control you had over your feelings. If you saw family money laying around or you did not want to wash for days or your temper flared up with jealousy and rage at your brother or sister, what was going to stop you from taking the money, from staying dirty, or from kicking and biting your brother or sister? Perhaps the only control you had was your training. You could hear the warning voices of your parents and others telling you what to do.

You needed your training.

But as you got older, your own inner personality that was waiting in the backstage of your being should have taken over the managing of your feelings. It is a more natural you.

So, we must conclude that once you have

outgrown your childhood the better supervisor for your feelings is the inner you.

The Stage Is Set

Our task now is to give you a detailed picture of each of these forces. The better you understand them and give them their proper places in your life, the better you will achieve God's plans for you.

God has made you to be happy and he has instructions you must follow to arrive at that happiness. An essential part of those instructions is to put your feelings and training in their proper places. Valuable as they are, God did not make your feelings to be in the driver's seat of your personality. Nor does he want your training to be there. God has made and given you your own, unique personality to be in charge of you. That is what he wants you to do. That is what will best insure your happiness.

Questions

1. Are you a feeling person?
2. Suppose you came upon an old drunk sprawled out on a sidewalk. Would you be angry at him for being there? Would you be angry at yourself for having walked down that street and seen him? Would you be inclined to help him?
3. What do the voices of your training say about helping such a person? Would they call you a fool if you tried to help in some way?
4. Were you ever down-and-out and in need of help?
5. If your training and your feelings differ, which one should you listen to?

2
TRAINING —
PAINTING BY
THE NUMBERS

Trying to become the person your training wants you to be is like doing a painting by numbers.

With a painting by numbers, the outline is there and the colors to be used are clearly indicated. All you have to do is to be careful to stay within the outline and follow the colors indicated by the numbers.

The person you should be according to your training also has its outline and colors. They are indicated by the "dos" and "don'ts" and the examples of others that have been impressed on your imagination and recorded in your memory. All you have to do is to follow carefully each detail you were taught or saw. You will laugh, cry, approve of or disapprove of, do or not do certain things. If you do all of this exactly, you will not have to be afraid of being rejected. You will be considered a good human being and, in the framework of ordinary circumstances, you will fit into things without too much trouble. You will have a memorized answer ready for most of the problems that arise.

What Is Training?

Since we will be talking a great deal about training, it might be good to clear up what we mean by training.

Training is acting according to an outside set of directions. If you train your dog, he acts according to your directions, not his instincts. If you train your hair, it takes the position you determine it should take.

So training is acting according to a set of directions that comes from an outside force. That force is like a hand that grips and guides and, at times, forces a way of feeling, thinking, and acting.

How does that force come from the trainer? It mostly comes by way of a command, a suggestion, or another's example.

On the part of the person being trained, he knows he had better act in that way, or else. At least externally he must do what he has been told or taught. He does not have to understand what he is doing. He only has to do it.

So training is mostly copying or imitating what others dictate or do. Your feelings or lack of feelings do not count. If you can get feelings from what you are doing, that is fine. If you cannot, then you will have to settle for the satisfaction of pleasing others. If they are pleased, then you are supposed to be pleased.

Your Best Pose

So the person your training wants you to be is a combination of all the dos and don'ts and ways of acting of others.

In most cases these dos and don'ts and

examples of others will insist on your acquiring the better qualities of life. That means being good, intelligent, kind, hardworking, loyal, fair, good-looking, pure, honest, etc.

In some cases, if enough people are no longer paying any attention to certain qualities, those qualities might not be stressed or might even be dropped. Thus to be pure or honest is not required in certain circles. You might even be considered foolish if you are either.

But, in general, the person your training wants you to be is the *best* of everything that is respectable. It is like having a portrait painted of you or going to a professional photographer and having a number of poses taken of yourself. Which one will you choose to have enlarged or have copies made of? Your choice is spontaneous. You choose the one that would look most favorable to others.

Called an "Image"

Because the qualities of the person your parents and others want you to be are put together by the part of your brain we call your imagination, the picture that is produced is often referred to as your "image." It is the picture you imagine that others want you to be and will judge you by. It could also become the picture by which you judge yourself.

This term "image" can be confusing, so it might help to explain it a little better.

What happens is that your imagination forms a picture of you based on the information it has received. "Let me see, what exactly do the important people in my life want me to be and do?

What do they keep insisting on? When do they praise me and others the most? When are they the angriest at me and others?"

From all of this data your imagination forms a rather clear picture or image of what others feel and think you should be like. You are pleased when you become or act like that kind of person. You become frightened when you do not.

So the imagined person or the image of what you should be is directly hooked up to your nervous system. Even before you are consciously aware of it, your nerves are moving you to become like that imagined person.

Advantages

A good training from parents and teachers who are intelligent and mature offers you tremendous advantages.

Training is instant knowledge. All you have to do is copy carefully what you are taught or see and you are able to do things that took others years and even centuries to learn. It is like buying a ready-made dinner or pie. On your part you only have to heat it up and it is ready to serve and eat.

Obviously, some training is of greater value than others.

Training that teaches you a trade and how to make a living is very important.

Training that teaches you how to live is even more important. That is why down-to-earth psychology and good religious instruction, when they join hands, are so valuable. One helps the other. Psychology clears the ground of obstacles that could interfere with religion producing good fruit. We see any number of examples of this in the

New Testament where Christ shows himself both as a master psychologist and a genius religious instructor.

One example of this from the Sermon on the Mount is where Christ points out that we should clear away our own faults before trying to clear away the faults of others. "You hypocrite! Remove the plank from your own eye first; then you will see clearly to take the speck from your brother's eye" (Matthew 7:5). What Christ is pointing out here is the tendency that psychology calls "projection." We tend to project or see those faults of others that we have but do not see in ourselves. But when we point a finger at another, we point three fingers right back at ourselves.

So training or time-tested instruction that is sound can help you by sparing you a lot of painful, bitter experiences of having to learn everything for yourself.

Guidelines

How can you tell whether all the parts of your training are sound or not?

Christ gave us good a practical norm as any for testing the soundness of your training: ". . . for you can tell a tree by its fruit" (Matthew 12:33).

So if parts of what you were taught are based on a narrow-minded prejudice or a partial truth, the wear and tear of time will show it up. We see this with family maxims, superstitions, and exaggerations. For example, the rule or impression that a young woman should not leave and live away from home except to get married or enter a convent is an exaggeration based on the fear that only the presence of her family will keep her moral.

In a religious sense a rule of training is good if it truly helps you to find the will of God. Christ ran into most of his difficulties because a lot of the religious training of his time did not express God's will. Much of the training was composed of misleading rules that had been multiplied for purely human motives of pride or greed. "This means that for the sake of your tradition you have nullified God's word" (Matthew 15:6).

Some Disadvantages

But, as with "good news, bad news" jokes, besides the advantages, there are some serious disadvantages or difficulties attached to even good, sound training.

The most serious difficulty that training can create is the tremendous pressure it can put on you always to be at your best when you are with others. It is as if others are carrying a camera with them and you have to be sure they go away with a good picture of you. Did you smile enough? Did you look presentable? Did you say or do the "right" or "in" thing? Were the people you were with impressed with you?

If you are afraid that others did not go away with a favorable picture of you, you can find yourself putting yourself down for having been so stupid, unpresentable, or inadequate.

"What are they going to think of me?"

That is the question uppermost in your mind. You go back and review what you said and did and hope it was not as bad as the scolding voices in your head say it was, but it is doubtful that you will convince yourself that your "image" was not seriously tarnished or marred.

Does this sound like an exaggeration of what happens or could happen?

It is not.

"Inferiority Complex"

You can get an idea about how real and serious these difficulties are from the great number of people who complain of having an "inferiority complex."

What is an inferiority complex?

It is a down-and-out feeling about yourself that comes from failing to be the person your training wants you to be. You are not like the picture or image you imagine you should be. A part of you knows this and scolds you. "If you had only done this or said that, you would have come off OK. But you did not. Once more you were not good enough. You are never good enough."

What is really surprising about all of this is that it would be closer to the truth to say that you have a "superiority complex," rather than an inferiority complex. You can have such a need to be the superior person your training wants you to be that you are down on yourself when you are not. Although you probably do not realize it and are not responsible for it, your need to be so superior makes you a victim of pride. You have a complex or pride to be more perfect than you are capable of being.

Acting as Conscience

This need from training to give a good picture of yourself becomes extremely critical when the dos and don'ts of your training act as your *conscience*. They tell you what is "right" and "wrong," and they punish you in the name of God.

"What is wrong with allowing your training to act as your conscience?" you might ask.

There could be a great deal wrong with it.

First, your conscience should be more than the dos and don'ts of others. Your real conscience should be coming from the real you.

Second, what happens if different teachers or preachers teach or preach entirely different ways of acting in a situation? Which one do you follow? Do you follow the one who taught you first? Do you follow the one who is stricter? Do you follow the one who is most lax? What do you do while you are deciding which one to follow?

Third, what happens when there is no do or don't to cover a situation, or your situation? What do you do then? Must you maintain a direct line to an authority figure who is standing by to feed you answers? That would be terrible. So whether the authority figure is a professional psychologist or a clergyman, this dependent way of acting could be quite harmful.

Why So Perfect?

As you read along you might wonder, "Why does my training insist on my being so perfect?"

The reason why your training is so insistent on perfection is because that is how training works. When you train your dog, your orders must be followed exactly. Your training is only effective if it allows no exceptions. If you allow any exceptions, confusion will set in. Your dog must do exactly as you say.

It is the same way with the training of a child. For your training to be effective, it must be firm. Otherwise your child knows he or she can wiggle out of things. If you allow an exception once, then why not again and again?

So, if the training you have received wants top performance from you, that is what you feel you must give. If you do not give such a good performance, it could mean a disapproving look of hurt from important people in your life.

So the negative reason why most people try to live up to their training as exactly as possible is to avoid being criticized.

A more positive reason why people try to live up to their training is to win the approval of others. If you love someone, you want to do the things that person approves of. That is normal. It can go to an excess, but the desire itself to want to please someone by doing exactly what he or she wants is not bad.

Examples

Marie was at a party with her husband. She hardly knew anyone, so she smiled and kept quiet the whole evening. She did not dare speak to anyone other than her husband for fear she would not be interesting or say the right things. Everyone thought she was shy. She accepted that. That was less embarrassing than being found dull or dumb. Actually, she would have liked to be the life of the party, but she was too frightened to attempt that. As long as she did not attempt it, secretly she could imagine herself as being that. She could believe that she was giving off a favorable impression or image of herself.

Steve was prematurely bald. He wore a hat everywhere he could, and when he could not, he avoided people and situations where some comment could be made about his receding hairline. Being prematurely bald did not go with the handsome image his parents and society wanted of him. Why did he not wear a toupee? Even that did not go well with his image. People who knew his condition would make jokes about him. He was stuck with his baldness and it cost him dearly.

Ann was always overweight. Her image of herself called for a thin person, but she was not able to fashion the trim figure expected of her. In a sneaky way, it was easier for her to accept being overweight because she was not trying than it would have been to try and fail. She could still hide behind the excuse that she was not really trying. She told herself that she could do it, if she put her mind to it.

William left job after job. Everyone said that he was intelligent. Why, then, could he not hold onto a job? Was he just lazy? It could seem that way. But if you knew anything about William and his training to be a success, you knew that he was frightened off by the fear of failing. So, before he advanced to any serious position of responsibility, he felt it was better to leave with a good record than take the chance of running into something he could not handle. By leaving while he was ahead, he could still hold onto the perfect picture he had of himself.

The Problem Is Old

The same problem of people trying to be the perfect persons their training wants them to be confronted Christ in his dealings with some of the people of his times.

Some of the Pharisees of his day felt that they alone knew the law and were living up to it. Everyone else was seen as a sinner or of little or no account. In one of his parables Jesus has one of the Pharisees saying, "I give you thanks, O God, that I am not like the rest of men — grasping, crooked, adulterous — or even like this tax collector. I fast twice a week. I pay tithes on all I possess" (Luke 18:11). Because of their self-righteousness Christ strove to break through to them.

Christ saw through these Pharisees. He knew that most of what they did was for "show." He could not stand their phoniness. He used some pretty strong language against them. Perhaps his best-known description of them was when he called them whited sepulchers. They looked fine on the outside, but inside they were filled with the corruption of the dead.

The truth is that much of Christ's teaching was to attack those who assumed they were special because they were doing or had more than others. Christ did not agree with them. Obviously he was not opposed to the good they were doing. Rather he was opposed to the smugness and the showing off that prompted them to do these good things. They were using religion to come off looking good to themselves and others. As we would say in this chapter, they came off with a good image or picture of themselves. They were doing all the things their training said they should, so they were satisfied with themselves. They assumed that God was also satisfied with them.

Was he?

Hardly. Christ tried to show them that God who is truth itself could not be satisfied with such phoniness. He used every means possible to show them the big mistake they were making, but they could not see it.

The Endless Parade

The parade of Marie, Steve, Ann, William, the Pharisees, and others is endless. They are all marching in dress parade for others to see them and approve of them. Whether they realize it or not, they are afraid to show pictures of themselves that are not their best poses. Something inside of them will not let them. They remember the times they took chances and failed to meet the approval of others. They felt so embarrassed and mentally beaten for having been so foolish. How would they be able to face others after what they did?

In our society people spend excessive amounts of money on clothes, cars, houses, and trips they really do not need and often cannot afford. Why do they do this? They do it to advertise what a success they are. For a time they come off looking good. They can even be the envy of others. How will they pay for all this advertising? They could pay for it with high blood pressure, middle-aged heart attacks, ulcers, etc.

In the area of mental health, it is difficult to count all the people who undergo "nervous breakdowns" because they cannot be the persons their training would want them to be. They are under such a strain to be what they are not but feel they must be, that they fall apart. Their nervous systems find it almost impossible to control their fears and rage over being failures and objects of ridicule.

In the area of alcoholism, many get their start from trying to live up to imaginary pictures of what they should be. If they are unsure of their performance, a first drink promises to calm them and give them confidence. A second drink is to make sure. A third drink could put them over the line of caring what happens or what others think of them. If they rely on alcohol to this extent, they could find themselves using drink as their way of handling pressures and problems. To rely on alcohol as a life support is to be an alcoholic.

Also, in the area of suicides, the need to be the "good" person that training wants has claimed many victims. Failing to be such persons, many cannot live with the punishment their minds put them through. Death seems like the only way out. Unfortunately, many take this solution rather than look for a better way to cope with life.

Although there are other serious difficulties or side effects to training, we will consider only two more, a need for excuses and a loss of freedom.

A Need for Excuses

Instead of accepting it when you have performed poorly, the tendency is to wipe away your poor performance by making excuses

Why is this?

Since those who trained you *assumed* you could carry out their dos and don'ts, you could find yourself assuming the same. So, then, why did you not perform better? Were you lazy, neglectful, or rebellious? If you were, then your poor performance is a matter of guilt.

How will you free yourself from this guilt?

The only thing that might save you is if you can prove that you did not know that you were supposed to act in a particular way or that some overpowering obstacle prevented you. This might excuse your poor performance.

Because these are the only reasons to excuse you from guilt, it is unbelievable how many tricks and how much energy you can spend trying to convince yourself and others that you *did not know* or *were not able* to stop what happened. We will consider two rather extreme examples to help make this clearer.

Did Not Know

Judy was married fifteen years before she found out that her husband had been unfaithful for most of their marriage. She became outraged when she found out. "What kind of an animal are you?" she attacked him. "Didn't you have any respect for me, your children, or yourself?" The verbal beating was ruthless and endless.

One day, after listening to her assaults against her husband, I said to her, "Judy, sometimes the only way we can understand why people do certain things is to try to see them from their point of view." It was not much more than a passing statement.

John, Judy's husband, started to consult me to see what he could do to save his marriage. Many sessions and several months later, John came in frustrated and angry. "Do you know what she has done? Judy has been having an affair and she does not feel the least bit guilty over it. She said you told her to do it so she could understand why I did it. She says you said it was all right."

I shook my head in disbelief. After a few moments I was able to explain what had happened. "Judy did a good job of quieting the guilt voices in her head. She told herself that an authority figure said it was OK, and that made it right. At least that was a good enough reason to plead ignorance of knowing that she was doing something wrong."

Could Not Help It

Janet was married to a man old enough and disinterested enough in her sexually to be her father. He was away every weekend.

One weekend Janet invited a male friend over for dinner. Janet looked stunning in the new outfit she bought for the occasion.

As the night went on, dinner gave way to dancing and dancing gave way to intimate touches. In a quiet voice Janet told her friend, "Take your one hand and hold my two hands behind me. Then I won't be able to stop you."

In Janet's mind, she had set up an excuse that would silence her guilt. "What could I do? He had pinned my hands behind me."

It was terribly sad that Janet had to play such games with herself.

The Real Harm

The real harm from making excuses is that it focuses all your attention on finding a way out of guilt. You are not concerned with the harm your actions have done to yourself and others. No, you are only concerned with getting rid of or avoiding the uneasy guilt feelings attached to such actions.

Does such a way of acting make sense?

It would not seem so.

Guilt is an alarm system to warn you that something is not right. To turn off the alarm without investigating what is wrong is foolish. If there is harm coming from what you have done, you should take a good look at that harm. If there is nothing wrong in what you have done, but the alarm of guilt is going off inside of you, then such a faulty guilt system should be corrected.

So, making and looking for excuses to justify your poor performance does not accomplish anything. It is a buy-off of guilt. It is not coming to terms with reality. In our examples of Judy and Janet, both of them did things that need examining, not excusing. Was Judy any more mature than her husband? Should Janet do something about her marriage or herself? Should both of these women go for help to straighten out their lives? These are questions that need real answers.

A Loss of Freedom

The other difficulty or side effect of training we want to consider here is the possible loss of freedom.

On one hand, your training helps you to assure your freedom by helping you to avoid a number of mistakes. Doing things in "tried and proven" ways eliminates a lot of sticky consequences that can come from acting impulsively.

On the other hand, while guarding against the carefree and careless tendencies of your feelings, your training can unnecessarily restrict your feelings.

Depending on how strictly and fearfully it was

imposed, your training can interfere with your freedom to act, to feel, and even to be.

If the dos and don'ts of your training stand like fierce, armed guards over your actions, then you will do automatically what they say.

If your training penetrates into your feelings like dye into cloth, it might control what you can feel and cannot feel.

If you completely identify with the person your training wants you to be, then you are not free to be your real self.

In each of these cases you could suffer a restriction of freedom that ranges from a partial loss to a total loss.

As a Consultant

The right way for your parents and teachers and for you to look on training is that the dos and don'ts of training are like a book of reference. It can be a good book of reference or a poor one.

As we have seen, it can be a good book of reference if it puts you in contact with the reality of God, with good ways of relating to others, and with good ways of relating to yourself. It is especially good if it shows you how to deal constructively with your anger, sexuality, greed, jealousy, etc. without destroying them.

It is a poor book of reference if it impedes your going out to God, to others, and to yourself realistically.

In a few words, we can say that the dos and don'ts of your training are like your own private library. Microfilmed on your memory is a book or a way of acting that covers almost all the areas of your life. It is all catalogued there, not in alphabetical order, but by association. As soon as you are about to do something, your memory gives you a "do" or "don't" to cover the situation.

So, your training is a valuable source of information which you should listen to and use when it fits. It can help by giving you rules and ways of acting that spare you the need to feel everything through here and now. That can be an immense help, especially when you are confused and need a solid way of acting.

But your training and the person it wants you to be is not the real you. It is too general and too much from others to be the person you really are. We must look elsewhere for the real you.

Questions

1. What kind of training did you receive as a child and adolescent? Do you approve or disapprove of it?
2. How has your training helped you? How has it hurt you?
3. Are you a victim of your "image"? Do you overworry and overanalyze your actions or another's criticism of you?
4. Were the Pharisees of the Gospel accounts victims of their images? What success did Christ have in teaching them his new and better ways of dealing with God, themselves, and others?
5. What was the most embarrassing experience you ever had? How did you live with yourself after it happened? Does it still bother you from time to time?
6. How would you teach training to others?

3
FEELINGS —
A ONE-SIDED
PORTRAIT

Since the person your training wants you to be is not the person God created you to be, where do we look for the real you?

Although in our first chapter we indicated that your feelings are not the real you, they have such a powerful influence over you and are so often mistaken for your real personality, it is worth our efforts to study them closely.

We will start our examination of your feelings by considering some of the characteristics they would want you and others to have.

The two most outstanding qualities your feelings want of you are that you act *lovingly* and judge *fairly*

Acting Lovingly

The fundamental belief of your feelings is that everyone should act lovingly. People should care and help one another so that no one ever goes wanting. Someone, somewhere, somehow should be able to fix things so that everything works out happily for everyone.

If everyone acted lovingly, the world would be a good world and evil would not exist. Work would be what you want to do. The beautiful things discovered by the sensitive intelligence of poets would be a big part of life, not just highlights.

In a few words, the world would be free of suffering. No one would be hurt or have to hurt others. Wars would not exist. Our English word for such a world is the word "innocence." This comes from the Latin words "not hurting." Your feelings would want and work for a world of innocence.

What about your hurtful or destructive feelings of anger, jealousy, and hatred? Should they be a part of life? Your idealized feelings respond: No, they should not exist.

Judging Fairly

What would protect this world of innocence which is the fundamental belief of your feelings?

This loving, caring world of your feelings would be insured if everyone judged things fairly.

Fair and unfair are big words for your feelings.

What is fair and what is unfair?

The idea of fair and unfair is based on simple justice. It is a kind of justice where everyone is treated the same and where you repay the same amount you receive. If you help someone with his problems, he should be willing to help you with your problems. If you give a gift or make a sacrifice for another, it is fair that you get a gift back and that he make a sacrifice for you. If you are honest with another, he should be honest with you. To use "double talk" would be unfair.

For all practical purposes your feelings would make what is fair or unfair the same as what is right or wrong. For your feelings, it would be wrong for a person to do anything that is unfair. A parent would be wrong if she gave one child more than another. According to your feelings, the owner of the vineyard of the Gospel story was wrong in giving those who worked the whole day in the hot sun the same wage as those who only worked one hour or two.

In a similar way it would be unfair or wrong for a person to die young. It would only be fair and right for a very old person to die, if he died painlessly in his sleep.

What would happen if someone has been unfair to you? Would it be wrong to be unfair to him? You could be unfair but only to the same degree. You would not be guilty because you would be making things even. You would only be guilty if you paid the other back too much.

When Disillusioned

So this loving, always fair person is the kind of person your feelings want you and others to be. With a world full of such wonderful people, it would be a wonderful world.

What happens when you find out that the world, your world, is not filled with loving, fair people? How do you protect yourself? There are too many to get back at each one personally.

You can react to your disillusionment in several ways.

You can feel so sorry for yourself that, as we will see later, you take off and hide in a place called "nowhere."

Or you can carry on your own private war of resistance by always being on your guard. As soon as you hear a harsh tone of voice or see an angry face, everything inside of you tightens up. Regardless of what that person has to say or teach and regardless of what it costs you, you want no part of him or her.

Not a Bad Picture

Setting aside what can happen because of disillusionment, the person your feelings want you to be is not a bad picture of you.

It is a picture of a natural you that is spontaneous with your likes and dislikes and with your judgments of what is fair and unfair.

It is a picture of a you that always wants to surface no matter how much it has been forbidden or held down by your training. You feel an emptiness and tension when it cannot surface.

So, the person your feelings want you to be is a rather nice picture of you. It is not the stiff portrait picture of your training. Its only drawback is that it is a one-sided portrait of you. It catches only the side of your feelings. It does not take into account your intellect, willpower, or you as a whole person.

You have feelings.

You are not your feelings.

The real you is something so much more.

A Source of Information

If your feelings are not the real you, what are they? What purpose do they serve?

God gave you your feelings to supply you with information and power.

First, your feelings have been assigned to your body to help you survive. They tell you in terms of pleasure and pain what will help you survive and what will not. Pleasure indicates that what you are doing is helpful, at least for a part of you. Pain indicates that it is not.

This needs explaining.

God has attached pleasure to the natural, basic functions you need for survival. The pleasures are a come-on to eat, sleep, eliminate waste products, keep warm in the cold, and engage in sexual activities.

The same is true of pain. When a basic function is ignored, abused, or attacked, you feel pain. If you eat too little, too much, or the wrong things, you get a stomachache. If you break a bone or are inflicted with devastating cancer that is attacking a vital organ, you are in excruciating pain.

This is on the physical level.

On the psychological level, the same things happen. A sense of pleasure comes from good order, inner peace, and worthwhile accomplishments. Pains that will not go away come from disorder, conflicts within your feelings, and frustration.

Regardless of the level, your feelings have a great deal to tell you, and it is worth your efforts to listen to them.

A Source of Power

Second, your feelings are an important source of energy.

Your feelings, in going after what is pleasurable and trying to avoid what is painful, release a tremendous amount of energy in your body. This should happen naturally and simply, but if your training or some other powerful fear interferes with the spontaneous functioning of your feelings, this energy is not released or it is blocked off before it arrives at the conscious level. It is trapped energy that makes you feel like you want to explode.

Perhaps a consideration of a strong feeling can help make this clearer.

Take a reaction that is common to everyone — fear. Regardless of why you are afraid, what will you do with your fear?

Will you deny that you are afraid because you do not want such ugly or cowardly feelings to exist? Or will you admit that you are afraid and let your fear prepare your body with the alert tension you might need to do something about the evil that is threatening you? Will you use the energy to run away, or will you put on the brakes, get angry, and stand and fight?

Depending on whether your feelings are free to register and release their energy or not, you will or will not have what you need to handle a situation.

If your feelings are not free to register and release their power, then you could run into a lot of complications. We will touch on a few of those complications.

Pushed Down Feelings

No matter why you do it, suppressing or pushing down your feelings can make you weak, drained, and depressed. We will take these reactions one at a time.

If your feelings were never developed, they cannot produce their effects. Like the empty gas tank of a car, your available fuel is zero. Where there should be power, there is weakness.

Worse than feeling "weak" is to feel "drained," because the energy needed to hold back such strong feelings of fear, jealousy, hatred, and anger is enormous. It is like the defense program of a country. The resources that could have gone into making your life better are poured into a defense program. That could be very costly and draining.

Perhaps the worst effect of all is the "pressed" down or depressed feelings you experience from pushing down such dynamic forces.

So, the weakness, the feeling drained, and the depression you often feel could be coming from cutting off your feelings before they have had a chance to make their reports and release their energy.

The Place Called "Nowhere"

Going a step further, if you have learned to cut off your feelings so well that you do not feel at all, you know of the secret hiding place called "nowhere." It is the suspended place where nothing bothers you because you do not feel what you should feel or because you are not in touch with what you are feeling. You are above your feelings. Like an airborne kite, you float above the pain of disappointment, failure, loss, or shame. Only a string keeps you in contact with what is happening around you

How did you learn to detach yourself from your feelings?

Perhaps you learned some of it from your training. If you were crudely trained, you were frightened into not feeling. "Don't you dare feel jealousy, hatred, anger, sex, or else." You felt and responded more to the fear of outside punishment or threat of rejection than to your inner, natural feelings.

Perhaps you learned a lot of it by yourself. After a number of times of being shocked and disillusioned because you felt you had been treated unlovingly and unfairly, you repressed your feelings of excitement over things. They began to retreat and became indifferent or not-caring. More and more, floating to the top of your consciousness, came the words, "I don't care. I don't care."

At first it was hard not to care, because underneath a part of you did care and would always care. But after awhile it began to work. You did not feel any pain when someone did not care about you or was unfair to you. Without realizing it, you had discovered the hiding place "nowhere." It was the place where you could have the world the way you felt it should be, your way, and without pain.

If this method of not feeling happens on a regular basis, a time will come when this retreat begins to take place automatically. Neither you nor others realize how much of the real you is stored within you. You know and they know that you can be distant at times or that you are not a very feeling person, but routine and memorized answers usually get you by. You are able to manufacture the feelings or responses you think the situation requires. If at times you are dissatisfied with your lack of feelings, you tell yourself that your feelings run deep and that is why they do not show easily.

In part, your answer is true. Your feelings do run deep. They are hiding in your retreat of "nowhere" or not feeling. They will not come out until it is safe or you find someone you can trust. Even then they are on the alert to race back into hiding at the threat of danger.

An Example of Blocked Feelings

Julia is an only child.

To her parents, Julia was not only a ray of golden sunshine, she was the sun itself. Their lives rose and fell with her smiles and tears. Nothing was too good for her. Except for one thing, she could have whatever love or money could buy her. That one thing she could not have was her independence. Her parents had plans, good plans, for her.

Because of all the love and good wishes they had for her, Julia knew she must never get angry at her parents and their restricting of her freedom. That would hurt them too much. It would in turn hurt her because she knew how sincerely they loved her.

So, Julia never got angry at her parents and their plans for her, except when she could not help it because something went crazy inside of her. Immediately after such blowups, she apologized and begged their forgiveness. She promised it would never happen again.

Unfortunately, or fortunately, these scenes did happen again and again, and they became worse. Everyone involved became so upset and confused that something had to be done about it.

First Julia and then her parents went for counseling.

On the surface, this need for help seemed tragic. After awhile, it was seen as a blessing. Today Julia can express her anger in words. She does not have to run away inside of herself to the place called "nowhere" and wait for an anger buildup and explosion to free her. She can tell her parents when they are hurting her. In turn, they can tell her when she is being unfair and is hurting them. Because their feelings are out in the open and are expressed when they are felt, they can deal with them and with each other.

Your Feelings and the Real You

So, although your feelings, and especially your blocked-off feelings, play such an important part in your life, they are not your personality. They are not your real ego.

Perhaps a good way to describe the relationship between your feelings and your real personality is to compare your feelings to the huge oil deposits of a country. Without the oil, the country would be so much poorer. With the oil, the country is rich and important. So, in many ways, it seems that the oil is the country. But it is not. It is only a part of the country.

It is very much like this with your feelings.

With alert feelings, you are alive. Without alert feelings, you are dull and lifeless. If your feelings have been blocked off or are twisted too badly, they can destroy you or have you destroy yourself.

But, regardless of how important your feelings are, they are not you. They are too little to control you, because their ways of judging according to fair and unfair are limited. There are a lot of things in life that are unfair but not wrong.

Moreover, as much as you might wish it, everyone in this world will not always act in a loving way. You know this from your own experience. The hurts you have received make it clear. And when you find yourself wounded by some unloving action sometimes your feelings will urge you to repay in kind. As much as you might feel that such a reaction would only be fair, your basic honesty would not let you call such "getting even" a loving act. So, living by your feelings does not promote interior harmony but, rather, puts you in a bind. You experience the tension between your ideas of fairness and what it means to be a loving person.

Also, your feelings should not be allowed to control you, because they often take things that are happening to others as if they were happening to you. This could involve you in people's problems in ways that are very unhealthy. It leaves no space between you and them.

So the person your feelings want you to be is not your real personality.

Questions

1. What is the most unfair thing you have ever experienced? Did you do something to strike back? Did you feel guilty in getting even? Or did you turn the other cheek and not try to get even?
2. Can you listen to and feel for another's misfortune without being carried away and reacting to it as if it were happening to you?
3. Do you feel there is an island inside of you that no one has ever touched?

4. Do you have intense feelings for or against anyone? Is there a difference between intense feelings and deep feelings? For example, a rapist has intense feelings for what he is doing. Does that mean that he has deep sexual feelings for his victim?
5. Does feeling good mean more to you than doing or being good?
6. Do you confuse how you feel with whom you are? In other words, do your feelings count more than your personality?

4
A
FULL-LENGTH
PICTURE

Having considered the kind of person your training and your feelings want you to be, we are ready to consider the wonder of your real personality. This is not going to be easy. The truth is that it will take much of the genius you are capable of to understand what the genius of God created in making you.

It will also require you to slow down and take a good look at yourself. God has woven your real personality so finely into your being that you might miss it if you do not know what to look for. Besides, the dos and don'ts of your training and the likes and dislikes of your feelings can put up such a fuss and make so many demands on your attention that you will have to make a serious effort not to be fully occupied with them.

In a few words, outside of God himself, there probably is no reality more profound than the wonder of your real ego. So, do not be impatient if you have to read this chapter over several times before it makes any sense to you. We will take it slowly, step-by-step, to help you understand the greatness of the gift God has given you in giving you your real self.

Bringing You into Focus

A simple way to show that your real personality is different from your training and your feelings is to point out some of the obvious differences between them. We will start with the fact that as a human being you are able to think for yourself.

The person you are supposed to be according to your training is not someone who thinks for himself. Rather, you are supposed to act in a way that has been imposed on you from others.

The person your feelings want you to be does not think. It *feels* and judges according to what is pleasing or displeasing. It might use your ability to think to figure out a way to get as much pleasure as possible for the least amount of effort or pain, but, of themselves, your feelings do not think. Your feelings weigh things on the scales of fair and unfair, not on the basis of truth or right or wrong.

From where, then, does the ability to think — to form ideas, make judgments, and draw conclusions — come? It comes from you. It is a special kind of knowing that comes from the rational or spiritual side of you. So, you are not just *trained feelings* or a *trained animal*. You are much more.

This ability to think is only one difference between you and your training and feelings. Your willpower or ability to act differently from your training or feelings is another.

Your Real Ego

Before giving a description of your real ego, it might be good to point out that the word "ego" is simply the Latin word for our English word "I." The Italians use the word "Io." The Germans use the word "Ich." So your ego and your I are the same.

Perhaps you are wondering, "Why do you speak of my *real* ego or I? Do I have more than one ego? Is it possible for me to use the word "I" to refer to something inside of me that is not my real personality?"

Yes, you can use the word "I" to express different things. At one time it might be expressing your training; at another, your feelings; at still another, your real personality. Let us listen to some everyday speech to see this.

A lady says, "I must clean in a certain way or I will be down on myself." Here the word "I" expresses her training. Her training says that this room must be cleaned in a certain way or her ego will not stop its scolding.

A man says, "If I do not get that new sports car, I am going to be miserable." Here the word "I" expresses his feelings. His feelings insist that if he does not get that new car, they are going to throw a tantrum.

Another man says, "I have thought it through and I have decided to quit my job. I know that my training is against quitting one job before I have another, and I know that my feelings are going to act up because money is going to be scarce, but I am determined to do it and put up with the consequences." Here the word "I" expresses his real or whole self or personality.

So the word "I" can be used in each of these three ways, but its best use is when it expresses you, the whole person. When it is your training or feelings that are speaking, it is better to identify them as your training or feelings.

As a Whole Person

We are now ready to consider the profound but simple reality of your real personality.

What is your real ego, your real self? Who are you, really?

Your real ego is you extended throughout your entire being. It is what connects all of you together. Although you are made up of many different parts, they are all parts of you.

How does your real ego connect your parts together? It does so by awareness and control.

By way of your brain and nervous system, your ego is in touch with all of you. If your foot hurts or does not hurt, you can be aware of it. And you are aware of it belonging to *you*. *"My* foot hurts. *I* kicked the table."

In addition to this awareness, your ego is able to control your impulsive senses, appetites, feelings, and those parts of you that need supervision to function correctly. If you make up your mind and insist that your appetite for food is not going to go to excess, it will not. Your real ego has enough connection with the operations that supply you with food that you are able to keep them in line. "I will not eat that piece of cake."

Your real ego has this power to be in control, but if you are not aware of your real ego and the power it has, then your real ego is little more than a tag-along shadow. It is there but that is all.

Becoming Aware

So your real self is the oneness and wholeness you

can sense and are aware of with your entire being. It is not any particular part of you. It is all of you. "I am the *whole* me."

Maybe some illustrations can help here.

A dress is not any one piece of fabric. It is all of the fabric joined together. The dress is the *whole* thing. The dressmaker had a design in mind which guided her to buy and arrange her materials in such a way that they would achieve her original thought. It is that completed design, now present in the fabric, that makes a dress. (How well she was able to transfer her thought to the fabric is another consideration.)

A similar thing happens with you.

God has a picture of a completed you in his mind. That completed, whole you is the real you. Somehow God tucks his design of you into the tiny human cell that begins you. Immediately that design goes to work to form you.

Physically, after nine months, enough of you has developed for you to leave your mother's womb. It is not too long before your arms and legs are strong enough for you to do things and move about on your own. All of this has happened according to the plan interwoven within you.

But, continuing the working of that design within you, you have been accomplishing more than just developing physically. You have also been developing emotionally and intellectually. This design is still at work inside you to develop your awareness of yourself as a whole person.

Like a Circle

Perhaps the oneness and completeness of a circle can help illustrate that your real personality is your awareness of and control over yourself as a completed, whole person.

For a hundred dots to form a circle they have to be placed in such a way that each is the same distance from a center point. If one or several of the dots break away or are not the same distance from the center, you do not have a circle.

Your real ego is something like that. The design thread of your real ego is stitched into your whole being. That unbroken contact throughout your being is your real ego. If any part of you can go on its own and is allowed to act independently of the best interest of the whole you, then *it* is what you are aware of, and *it* takes over the control of you.

Getting Control

Hopefully, from these illustrations of a dress and a circle, it is a little clearer that some things are the whole thing, not the individual parts.

It is this way with your real ego. It is the whole you.

It is important for you to realize this.

It is equally important that you do whatever is necessary to achieve this wholeness and to-getherness with yourself. It is *you,* not some part of you, who should run your life.

How do you achieve this wholeness?

In a conflict with your appetites for food or drink or whatever, you can ask yourself who is going to win? Am *I* going to win, or is a part of me that has gone to excess going to win and take control away from me?

Put on this basis, you would have to be a very foolish person to let your appetite win. You might not be able to change things immediately, especially if some psychological factors of trying to achieve the good feelings of childhood are influencing your excessive eating or drinking, but you can begin to correct matters by taking some steps of going to Weight Watchers, Alcoholics Anonymous, or for therapy.

The power that comes from putting things on such a basis is immense. It is *you* — not your training — imposing a discipline on yourself. It is *you* — not parts of you — in control of you. A calm settles over you and you are at peace. The dos and don'ts of your training and the demands of parts of you will probably scream at you to have their way, but you are having it your way. You are in control of you, and this awareness makes you very grateful to God for having given you the gift of your own personality. You would not exchange it for anyone else's personality.

A More Mature Conscience

Once you realize this truth, that the real you is the whole you God has imprinted in you, it opens up other truths.

For one thing, it gives your conscience a more interior principle to operate on than the rules of your training. Remember, those rules come into you from others.

By measuring your actions from the principle — that this good is for me as a whole person — you have a say in your actions. You are not just a parrot or robot doing what others say you should. You are judging by what is good for the total you, body and spirit. "Yes, I want to eat, drink, engage in sexual activities excessively and without concern for others or tomorrow, but is this good for me as a responsible or religion-minded person?''

If your conscience judges your actions in this more mature way, then morality is more than artificially copying the dos and don'ts of others. It is also more than a game of trying to outsmart or to block off the dos and don'ts of your training. Right and wrong are determined by what helps or hurts you as a whole person who lives with others and is subject to God.

Before, Not After

If you learn to make moral judgments on the basis of how your action is going to affect you as a whole person, then you will want to make your judgments *before* you actually do a thing, not after. You want to know ahead of time how your action will affect you as a whole person and in your relationships with God and others. You are not interested in playing dumb or trying to escape the guilt attached to a bad action. No, you want to avoid the harm it will cause you and others.

So, the guilt or lack of guilt you attach to an action when you make your judgment is the guilt it has. The guilt cannot change because your action does more harm than you realized it would cause. You might decide differently about such a way of acting in the future, based on how it turned out or on new considerations, but that is in regards to future actions. It has nothing to do with the right or wrong of your present action. How you judged before you acted still holds.

A conscience based totally on the dos and don'ts of training also wants you to judge your actions before you act, but so often it waits to see how your action turns out before giving you a final verdict of guilt. If your action turned out OK, then you will probably feel the minimum of guilt. If your action does not turn out well, you will probably be anchored down with severe guilt. The memorized voices of your parents and other authority figures will turn on you and say, "You should have been more careful. You probably knew it was going to be bad, but you did not admit it to yourself. Anyway, regardless what you thought, you should be punished to make sure it does not happen again."

As someone has said so well about the conscience regulated by the dos and don'ts of training, "It is a *gotcha* conscience. It waits for you to make a mistake or come close to making a mistake. Then it preaches to you and you cannot stop it until you beg for forgiveness and promise it will never happen again."

A conscience based on what is good for you as a whole person does not act that way. It presumes that you are an adult and that you want to know what is good or bad for you. You do not follow it to buy off guilt.

Making Decisions

What applies to conscience and making decisions about guilt also applies to making other decisions.

If you always look to the direction and examples of others to show you what to do, you are missing out on important opportunities for growth. Each decision that you make on the basis of yourself as a whole person helps you to grow. If it is not a good decision, you will learn from it. If it is a good decision, you will grow in confidence in your abilities.

Making decisions about what is good for you as a whole person can occur in so many areas of your life that are not a matter of conscience. What job will you take? Whom will you marry? Where will you live? How much will you engage in social activities?

To procrastinate or make no decisions in such matters is bad. To make decisions solely on what your parents or others think you should do comes too much from the outside. To make decisions on how you feel at this moment is not stable enough. Somehow — it depends and varies with the kind of decision you have to make — what you think will be good for you as a whole person should come into your consideration and help you to decide what to do.

Interior Religion

This wanting what is good for you as a whole person is what underlies good religious instruction.

It is what underlies Christ's teaching.

We see Christ refer to it when he warns that if parts of your body want what is harmful to your whole body, then it is better to sacrifice the part. "If your right eye is your trouble, gouge it out and throw it away! Better to lose part of your body than to have it all cast into Gehenna. Again, if your right hand . . ." (Matthew 5:29-30).

Taking the same principle a little further, Christ says it is better to lose even your body if it is harmful to your spirit and you as a whole person. "I say to you who are my friends: Do not be afraid

of those who kill the body and can do no more"
(Luke 12:4).

Christ supports this statement with the truth
that has been quoted so often over the centuries,
"What profit does he show who gains the whole
world and destroys himself in the process?"
(Luke 9:25)

So we see that Christ directs his teaching
toward protecting and making you aware of
yourself as the whole person.

St. Paul adds to Christ's teaching by insisting
that "He is a real Jew who is one inwardly"
(Romans 2:29). The real Jew is the person who is
in contact with his real self, not just someone who
conforms to or carries out external laws.

The Open Road

Once you recognize the truth of your real self,
you have an open road to most other realities.

You have an open road to your own development. You are not restricted to the limitations of
training and your feelings.

You have an open road to others because you
can recognize the unique gift they are, even if they
are not aware of it. It is unlikely that you would do
anything to hurt them, because in doing so you
would be compromising your own dignity. You
are a person. You are not a wild animal. Besides,
if God is our common Father, to hurt another is to
hurt someone with whom you are related. That
would not make sense.

Most important, you have an open road to God.
You will want to know him and his truth and
goodness because he is the model of your truth
and goodness. And if you are fortunate enough to

realize that Christ is God, then you will want to know every aspect of Christ and make his life and teaching your own.

We will see more of your relationship and ways of relating to God in a later chapter. For now, we want to point out that the better you know your real self, the better you will know God and Christ. Your real self is not only capable of knowing God, it is eager to know its origin and final destination.

Summing Up

So mature decision-making about something important should take into account your training, feelings, and intellect. As each of these reports its case to you for consideration, you, the whole person, are in a better position to make a decision about what is best for you and others.

We will quickly run through what happens when you have an important decision to make.

As soon as you become aware of being involved in a situation that seems important to you, different parts of you rush in with their reports.

Your training informs you about what authority figures from your past and present life say you should or should not do in such a situation.

Your feelings, perhaps disregarding the threats of your training, are telling you what they want and do not want.

If your training and feelings are so strongly opposed to each other that you have an open fight on your hands, you might not get to the reports of your intellect. In such a case, the real you could be like a spectator waiting to see which side will win — your training or your feelings.

But, if you are not so caught up with the conflict

between your training and feelings, you can consult with your intellect and gain all the information necessary to make a good decision based on what is best for you as a whole person.

Perhaps for now it is best to follow your training or your feelings and put up with the complaints of the side you do not choose. Or you might have to wait until you have more information or growth to see what is really good for you.

Maybe the example of Elizabeth will help make this clearer.

Elizabeth

Elizabeth, a woman in her early thirties, has the enviable problem of having Anthony and Hugo interested in marrying her. Which one should she choose?

Anthony is in his late thirties. He is a gentleman. He dresses neatly, speaks well, and is on his way to becoming a successful broker on Wall Street. He is on time for his dates and takes her to the nicest places.

Hugo, who is Anthony's age, is an overgrown kid at heart. He has had a number of jobs but has not found one he really likes. Hugo is all feelings. He has an invisible way of getting inside of people. When he is up, and that seems to be most of the time, he is a circus. When he is down, he is like the leading character of a tragedy. He dies so convincingly.

Whom should Elizabeth marry?

On the one hand, her parents would love her to marry Anthony, but she cannot warm up to him. The truth is that he leaves her cold. Everything he does, even his smile, seems rehearsed. He has no spontaneous feelings. Of course she is pleased with his adoration and dependability, but is that enough for a marriage?

On the other hand, her parents have warned her about Hugo and what life would be like married to him. She knows they are right, but he does something to her feelings that she cannot even begin to describe. Just the thought of him excites her. To be with him is an adventure of unpredictability. He is like a revolving door; she can love him at one turn and hate him at the next. Depending on his mood, he can make her the luckiest woman or the most miserable woman in the world.

What is the mature thing for Elizabeth to do? Whom should she pick?

If she really thought it through, probably the mature thing for Elizabeth to do is to marry neither and wait for someone who is more balanced. Anthony seems caught up in so many dos and don'ts that he is almost without feelings. He is smart, but he is not warm. Hugo is a flood of undisciplined feelings. He is warm, but at times he is depressing to be with. Neither seems to have enough of his own real ego to be a whole person. It would not be good for Elizabeth who is trying to be a whole person to marry either.

Know Your Real Self

Although much time has been spent here in a negative way — to give you an awareness of your real self by showing you that your real self is *not* your training nor your feelings — in this chapter we have given you some positive considerations of what your real self is and what it can do. It has only been a sketchy outline of the real you, but it is a start. You will need a number of experiences where you think of yourself and act as a whole person before you get a solid grasp of your real self.

Once you recognize your real self and the unassuming power it gives you, you will not be able to settle for less.

You will not be deceived into believing that your physical appearance, clothes, wit, talent, and success — no matter how impressive — are the true goals of life. Such things are good, provided you do not live for them and judge your worth by them. Their "high" is nice, but because it is based on something to "show-off" it is too fragile to depend on.

Also you will not be deceived into believing that you live in a world of innocence where you can be carefree because nothing or no one should ever hurt you. Impulsive, thoughtless ways of acting, whether by you or others, can hurt you.

The design or drive inside of you to be a whole person will make you feel uneasy should you allow the *need* for success or carefree pleasures to dominate you. You will know that neither of these can take the place of your real personality.

Nor will you want to exchange your real self for anyone else. God has made your real personality special. You will know that you cannot improve on it. Being *your* real self, you will be as free and happy as a human being can be in this life.

Questions

1. Do you know any "real" people? Are most of the people you know copies of someone else?

2. Does a person have to be attractive, educated, or rich to be real?

3. Do you have a oneness or togetherness inside of you that comes from you or do you often feel you are falling apart?

4. What was the hardest decision you ever had to make? Were you scared? Did you consult others? Were you aware of your feelings? How did you finally decide what to do? Would you approach it differently today if you had to make that same kind of decision?

5. In art, what is the difference between an original masterpiece and copies of it? Are you working toward the original masterpiece God created you to be or have you settled for being a good copy of some adult who seems to be making it? Have you secretly decided to stay a child? Are you aware that the real you is the *whole* you? Are you confused over what it means to be real? Is there someone you can ask to get direction to help you understand who you really are?

5
ACCEPTING
ALL OF
YOU

Having seen that your real ego is when you are aware of yourself as a *whole* person, we want to see what should be your attitude toward the many and various parts of your being.

Here is a principle that seems too obvious for need of proof: Since an intelligent God has made you, all of you, each part of you has its own purpose for being. To block off or ignore the reports coming from your senses, appetites, and feelings is not right. Sooner or later, it has to have a bad effect on you.

Blocking off or ignoring unwanted, natural parts of your personality would be like throwing away pieces of a jigsaw puzzle because you do not see how they fit into the whole puzzle. To your regret, you will see later where they should have gone and how incomplete the puzzle is without them.

"But," you might object, "I don't like it when I get frightened, angry, hateful, and jealous. They are such ugly feelings and they make me feel and look so ugly. Besides, my religion and training do not want me to like them or my sexual feelings. I have been taught to deny them or get rid of them as fast as possible. I am to distract myself, say a prayer, or do whatever I must to get rid of them. So, how can these parts of me be good or important to me? What is more, I have invested so many years of my life trying to repress my anger out of existence that I do not know how to get angry. Do you mean this has hurt me? I do not understand what you are saying."

A Need for Understanding

Without a doubt, this acceptance of your whole self can be confusing and critical.

So much of the conflict between psychiatry and religion enters here. While religion seems to urge you to *suppress* yourself, psychiatry seems to urge you to *express* yourself. Religion says to hold back your animal nature. Psychiatry says to release it. Who is right?

Before we can answer this question of who is right, we must clear up a number of things.

First, realistic religion and balanced psychiatry do not take such firm sides. To say they do is to oversimplify. Some religious teachers and some psychiatrists might take such opposed positions, but they are speaking for themselves. They are not expressing the truths assigned to each group to teach.

Second, we are speaking about *listening* to all of your parts and the reports they have to make. We are not saying that you should do everything your appetites or feelings say.

It is like a free press. At times it is a nuisance and a danger for a country to have a free press, but in the overall picture it is good to know what is happening, even if some reports are lies or exaggerations.

In the same way God and nature have given you your appetites and feelings for very definite purposes. To destroy them or deny them is an insult to God. So if religion is speaking about God and his plans for you, it cannot tell you to destroy what God has given you. It can tell you to control it, but not to destroy it.

Benefits

As we considered in chapter 3, the positive benefits of listening to your senses, appetites, and feelings are enormous. They are like self-starting instruments that report the information and generate the power you need to cope with situations.

If you are faced with a danger, your body is quick with fear and the energy you need to run away or to stand and possibly fight.

If you are sexually attracted toward another person, all kinds of energy releases itself. You can be so vitalized that you feel you are going to burst.

If you are jealous of people who have more than you, you are given the awareness and desire to go out and get better things for yourself.

There are so many marvelous machines inside of your senses, appetites, and feelings that are ready to turn on and color your life with their special contributions if you let them.

An Objection and Answer

"But," you might be objecting, "these down-to-earth appetites and feelings have a destructive tendency to them. If they are allowed to go too far, they will destroy to get what they want. One look at newspaper headlines shows that. Besides, even if I do not allow them to destroy others, their mere presence destroys something inside of me. They destroy my sense of 'innocence.' Why do I have to live in a world where such feelings are necessary? They are too scary and too ugly to let them be a part of me. I don't want them.''

But you do live in such a world.

It is not a totally good world.

It is not a totally bad world.

It is a world of flowers and thorns — like our beautiful flower, the rose.

So there is a place in your life for innocence and there is a place for suspicion and caution. As Christ phrased it so well, ''You must be clever as snakes and innocent as doves'' (Matthew 10:16). As Christ suggested to his disciples before his capture — have your swords ready, even though you might not use them. We see a similar situation in our country spending so much of its resources for defense. Because we are strong, we do not have to use our weapons, but we have them available if we really need them.

Harms from Nonacceptance

One harm that comes from suppressing your feelings is the price you must pay to keep your feelings from surfacing. You always have to be alert to avoid situations that can bring on feelings of fear, anger, hatred, and sex. If that does not work, then you have to distract yourself away from what is happening by intellectualizing or generalizing things and situations. If neither of these work you might have to resort to drink or drugs not to feel or react to what is happening.

Closely connected to these costly procedures to avoid feeling is the possibility of finding yourself in the scary place we have described as "nowhere." Feeling nothing or next to nothing, you almost do not exist.

A second harm that can come to you from not feeling what you should feel is a tendency to concentrate on negative things in people and in life. Seeing all the bad there is in others helps you to avoid them and contacts with them that could bring on fearful, hateful, and sexual feelings. Unfortunately, since you are on the lookout for "negatives" in others and in life, you will not see the "positives" or "pluses" that are around you. Counting up only the negatives, you could establish a serious case of "poor me" and "how hard life has been to me." You are setting the trap to become a *self*-made martyr.

The Need for Honesty

So it is vital to listen to and accept the reports of your senses, appetites, and feelings.

What does it mean to listen to and accept their reports?

It means that they should be allowed to make their reports uncensored. If you feel afraid, you feel afraid. If you feel angry, you feel angry. If you feel sex, you feel sex. You have to be honest about what you feel.

"But all of this scares me. You do not understand. For me to feel these things is not such a simple thing. They make me feel guilty and uneasy. If I feel my fears, I just know that I am going to shrivel down to a very small person, and even to nothingness. Besides, if I let my anger out, I'm afraid I am going to hurt someone. As for my sexual feelings, forget it. They have gotten me into enough trouble in my life. Who needs them? So I have to distract myself or turn off my feelings to survive. I am really confused."

Your confusion is understandable. If you are not accustomed to thinking and acting as a whole person, then these powerful feelings are scary.

Control

So, there is a need to be cautious in dealing with these more dangerous feelings. Your guidelines for allowing them or encouraging them to surface depends on the amount of control you have over yourself. The more your whole ego is in control of you, the better you can handle and profit by the reports of your individual parts. If you have little control over your fears, anger, jealousy, and sex, then you will need to go slowly and probably seek help to let these dangerous feelings surface.

But, despite the dangers involved and your need to go cautiously, if you want to be a whole person, you must accept all of your feelings. Each has its own part to play in your life.

"What should I do when my feelings and appetites make their reports and generate their power?"

You should treat them like other vital forces of nature. You should harness them and put them to work for you as a whole person.

Thus your anger is like a mighty river. Its power can be destructive or constructive. It depends on how you use it. (Read the series, *You and the Ten Commandments,* by the author of this book.

Consult the fifth commandment.)

Your sexuality is a font of life within you. You can use it legitimately or illegitimately. It depends on you. (Read *Sexual Morality,* by the author of this book.)

So the winning attitude is *acceptance* and *control.*

To suppress vital forces God and nature have given you until they explode because they cannot be held back any longer is foolishness and a waste. But to be aware of and bring such forces under the control of your ego is to be truly human.

"But, what about the capital sins of anger, etc.? Am I not supposed to run away from them?"

You are not supposed to destroy or deny these valuable forces. You are expected to control them. They should not control you. They only become sins when they are allowed to take control of you.

The Right Way

So the reports of your senses, appetites, and feelings are important to you.

They tell you what is happening around you, and they prepare you to be able to respond to what is happening. Whether you choose to respond or not should be up to you, not up to your senses, appetites, or feelings. This is the way God planned it. There are other ways of acting, but this is the right way.

Does all of this seem too idealistic to be useful in daily life?

It could seem so. Most people are not aware of themselves as whole persons. As we have said, they are what they feel at the moment or they are who their training says they should be.

Although this is probably true, it should not be so.

If this is how you have thought of yourself, maybe this is your time to change. Rather than be dominated by the perfect image your training demands or by your impulsive parts, maybe you can begin to think of yourself and live your life as a *whole* person.

Questions

1. Is all of you good or did God make parts of you bad?
2. Would you rather live in a world of "innocence" where no one would have the freedom to hurt anyone, or do you prefer the challenges of the world you live in?
3. In this matter of accepting your whole self, is there a real conflict between good psychiatry and realistic religion?
4. Is there a connection between modern sexual excesses and the severe training concerning sex of a century ago? What should be a proper attitude toward your sexuality?
5. Have you ever been severely depressed? Did you realize that you were depressed because you were pressing down your anger so as not to feel it or express it?
6. What do you do when you get jealous of someone? Can any good come from feeling jealous of another's success?
7. Are you honest with yourself about your feelings? Do you have a friend with whom you can share your feelings?

6
TOO
MUCH
"I"

As you have been reading along, has something been bothering you? Have you felt an uneasiness over all the importance given to you, to your ego? Have you felt that to spotlight yourself so much is selfish, unchristian, and wrong? Is it not an *ego trip* at its worst to be so wrapped up with yourself? Besides, does this not go against Christ's teaching of denying and emptying yourself?

Reasons for Confusion

If you are confused over all the attention this book has given to discovering and developing your real self, your confusion is understandable. This approach of concentrating on your real self is different from what you have been taught. The "big" people in your life condemned giving yourself too much attention or importance. Their strongest disapproval of you would be to say, "You are selfish. You don't think of anyone but yourself."

At first glance the same seems true of Christ. His constant theme was to do for others. "Treat others the way you would have them treat you:

this sums up the law and the prophets" (Matthew 7:12).

"So," you might question, "if so many teach that my success as a human being depends on what I do for others, does that not go against what I am reading here? I do not understand it."

Unfortunately, your confusion is understandable and regrettable. There has been a great deal of confusion over what it means to love yourself. How can you love yourself without being selfish and self-centered in a bad way?

Dispelling Confusion

There is a door out of this confusion.

The "I" or ego that your parents, teachers, preachers, and Christ are attacking is not your real self. They are attacking either the false, over-perfect person the dos and don'ts of your training could lead you to believe you should be or the careless, irresponsible you of your impulsive feelings. Both of these need attacking.

If you have confused yourself with the over-sized person your training wants you to be then you need to be cut down to size. Christ's problem with some of the Pharisees of his time was precisely over this. Because they prayed, fasted, and gave alms more than others, they got carried away with themselves. They concentrated so much on showing off a "good image" of themselves that they did not see how small and bigoted they really were. Christ tried to deflate them, but they would not be deflated. They ended up killing him.

The same could be true if you have confused yourself with the impulsive you of your feelings.

So often your feelings want to be immediately gratified, especially if they have been deprived for a long time. They want what they want when they want it. Obviously such an impulsive way of acting, that wants everything that catches and pleases your eyes, needs to be trimmed and denied.

In both of these cases of false you or impulsive you, a going out to others could help keep them in line. However, there is no guarantee that it will, because your helping others could feed your already exaggerated importance and could set your feelings up to expect and demand a reward for all that it has cost you to help others.

Making It Clear

So you cannot give too much importance to your real ego. The more you are your real ego, the more you will be able to do as Christ says, "Love your neighbor as yourself" (Matthew 19:19). This means that true love of others cannot happen if you do not love yourself.

But let us make it very clear that when we use the words *your real ego*, we do not mean what is commonly understood as *your ego*. In everyday speech the word "ego" usually refers to the person your training wants you to be.

Thus we say of another who praises us, "Come around more often. You are good for my *ego*." Or we say of someone who criticizes and condemns us, "Boy, she really flattened my *ego*. I felt like I would sink into the ground."

The ego referred to in these statements is what we have called your "image" or the personality you want to show in front of others so that they will accept you. It is what is meant in the expression — to take an ego trip.

Yes, when this exaggerated ego runs you, beware. It wants your name in neon lights for everyone to see, acknowledge, and remember. It wants and needs you to be *number one*. It could drive you unmercifully to gain this recognition, and it can get you to explode angrily at anyone who interferes with your attaining it.

As we have pointed out, this exaggerated ego is not what we mean when we speak of your real ego.

By discovering and developing your real self, you are really loving yourself. Sharing this you with others, you profit and so do they. (Read *Love Yourself* by Edward Richardson, M.M., available from Liguori Publications).

Questions

1. What does the word *ego* mean to you? When you say "I," what does it mean? Is it referring to your training, to your feelings, or to yourself as a whole person?
2. Can you have a fair discussion with a person who is trying to protect or exalt the over-exaggerated ego of his training? Will he want to have the last word, even if it is said under his breath or to himself?
3. If a person really blows up at you, which ego is directing him?
4. Is Christ against you loving your real self?

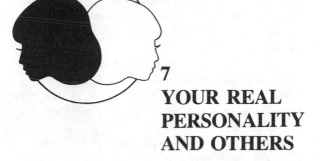

7
YOUR REAL PERSONALITY AND OTHERS

As we have seen, concentrating on your real personality is not wrong or unchristian. And it is absolutely necessary if you want to have a healthy relationship with others.

Because other people play such an important part in your life, we will consider in this chapter how you can relate to others. We will divide our consideration according to the three stages of being *dependent*, *independent*, and *interdependent*. As we describe each of these stages, you can see where you presently are and some of the possibilities of where you could be.

As Dependent

Everyone starts life as a dependent person. We need others. Without them we could not survive. That is natural.

If, after we have grown up, we still need others to survive, we continue to be dependent. That is not so natural.

A dependent person is like a ladder leaning against a building. With the support of others, the dependent person is capable of climbing quite high. Without their support, he can do very little. The dependent person can daydream great things, but he cannot make those dreams real. Something always stops him.

A person, you, can be dependent on others because of *natural* or *social* needs.

Some of the natural needs that others can provide for you are food, clothing, shelter, and medicine.

Some of the social needs they can provide are friendship and support in facing difficult tasks and status.

But regardless of the need, if you are a dependent person, you cannot act alone. You need others. The need might be neatly covered over, but if the support of some important person in your life is taken away, then you are not capable of coping alone.

This depending on others to provide for a need is how most people relate to one another. They satisfy mutual needs. When one or both no longer have or can supply a particular need, it could be the end of their relationship.

The Example of Joe and Ruth

You can see some of this need-relating in the case of Joe and Ruth. Joe goes to medical school and spends most of his time studying. Ruth, his wife, goes to work to help pay off the bills.

Joe needs Ruth.

Ruth needs Joe.

Joe becomes a doctor.

As an established doctor, Joe no longer needs Ruth's financial help. He has become so successful that he does not even need her encouragement and moral support. The truth is that Joe has outgrown the needs that Ruth once fulfilled.

What is going to happen to Joe and Ruth?

If their relationship never progressed beyond needs, Joe and Ruth could find that they have no relationship, except that of their children or a sentiment for the past. Neither of these might be enough to keep them together. If they have not or cannot learn to appreciate and love each other as independent individuals, it could be the end of their marriage.

As Independent

If in growing up you have become an independent person, *ordinarily* you do not need others. You are able to take care of yourself. You can do things, go places, come up with your own ideas, and keep your fears and frustrations from getting the best of you.

In extraordinary cases of serious sickness, legal trouble, or betrayal, you might need to turn to others, but that is because of the exceptional circumstances that have hit you and knocked you down. Once you have recovered from the knockout blow, you are ready and able to take back your independence.

So to be independent means that you have grown up enough to be your own person. You could and do rely on others, but ordinarily you do not have to. It would take something away from you as a person or your relationship with another if you had to lean on him or her because you never learned to be independent.

A few words of caution might help here. Do not

confuse being independent with being *isolated*. Such people can look alike, but they are vastly different.

Like an independent person, an isolated person also prefers to do things on his own. He *pretends* not to need anyone. The truth is that he needs people, but he is afraid to go out to others because they might reject or dominate him. He feels very uneasy when he finds himself getting too close to others or that they are getting too close to him. A panic alarm goes off in him and he consciously or subconsciously begins to withdraw from others.

So there are big differences between being isolated and being independent. Although at a glance they look the same, they are not. As Christ would say, ". . . you can tell a tree by its fruit" (Matthew 12:33). The following examples of Ralph and Todd make this clearer.

Independent Ralph, Isolated Todd

Ralph is thirty. He is a graduate from the school of hard knocks. He is also a graduate from nursing school. He was one of the first male nurses in his hospital.

When Ralph made up his mind to do something, he did it. What others thought of him was important and so were his feelings, but neither was as important as his awareness that he was his *own* person and that he was a *whole* person.

Ralph was often misunderstood by his parents and others. He was often confused himself. Despite the misunderstandings and confusion, he would not settle for anything less than to be a real person. He did not always succeed at it, but he tried.

Todd was an exceptional child. He had the over-alert imagination and sensitivity common to a person subjected to fear at a very early age.

By the time he was six, Todd was a professional con artist. His excited eyes and pleasing smile over a gift just made you want to give him things. Everyone liked and had high hopes for him.

But something was wrong. Underneath those excited eyes and winning smile, Todd was not smiling. He hurt easily. He had a secret fear of being abandoned. He was not always aware of it, but he felt its sickish emptiness every time someone hurt him.

Although Todd surfacely went out to a lot of people, he had no close friends. This gave him the appearance of being independent, but he was not. He really was a very isolated person.

Being Responsible

A good way to separate the independent person from the dependent person is to say that the independent person accepts his life as his own. The dependent person does not; rather he plays the game of "follow the leader." Someone else is given the responsibility for his life and decisions. For all practical purposes he is still in his mother's womb. He is too scared of life to leave.

It might be in order here to point out that we are not condemning anyone who is hanging onto others for support. This book is not out to condemn. It wants to help. However good the reasons for being dependent seem, it is costing the dependent person and everyone associated with him too much. The investment of clinging is not worth the false security it brings.

So the independent person wants to be responsible for his own life. He does not want to be *overburdened* with his own responsibilities or with those of others. If he needs help, he will ask for it. If others need help, he will give it. But he will not take over or live another's life. He values his own independence too much to deprive himself or others of it.

As Interdependent

So your real ego wants to relate to others independently. Instead of needing other people, you want them. You feel that relying on others to take care of you or make you feel popular and important is *using* them. It is treating them like things, not people.

But to want others because of their feelings, intelligence, and goodness is to appreciate them for themselves. You can go out to them without paying the inflationary price of dependency. You keep a respect for yourself and for them.

This kind of relating with others is an *interdependency*. You accept the challenge to be with another so that you can share yourselves with each other.

In closing off this section, we see that the independent person can be alone without being lonely. The truth is that he is rarely alone. He wants to go out to others, and they enjoy the experience of his company.

In Search of Answers

If it is normal to go from being dependent to independent to interdependent, why do so few accomplish it?

Many have tried but failed to answer this *seemingly* simple question, but it has no simple answer. It is a question with a number of parts, which must be examined before an answer can be given.

What are these parts?

First, who makes a person independent? Does he do it on his own? Do others do it for him? Is it a combined effort on the part of the individual and others?

Second, how do the past and present enter into his development? Does a person have to go back and straighten out or fill in voids from his past before he can become independent? Can he skip the past and concentrate on "now" and assert his independence?

As you can see, we are dealing with a number of important questions. Too many parents have laid heavy burdens of guilt on their consciences because they felt they must have failed in bringing up their children. Many sons and daughters have hated and blamed excessively their parents because they were allowed to grow up incapable of coping with life.

So we will step cautiously as we try to answer these difficult questions. We will start by indicating the kind of influence people have had in your becoming an independent person. We will then proceed to consider — if you have not become an independent person — what you can do *now* to help you become such a person.

Your Formation

At the beginning of your life and for a considerable time after, your parents and others play a very important part in how you will develop.

If your parents and others are sensitive, independent people who have found themselves, they will want the same independence for you. By their example and actions they will direct you between the mountains of your training and your feelings. They will encourage you to be your real self.

If your parents and others — perhaps through no fault of their own — are not sensitive, independent people who have found themselves, then there can be trouble. If you try to become independent, it could be seen as a danger to yourself and others. They will probably feel that they have to crush this wild streak inside of you by laying a mountain of dos and don'ts on you. Thus, instead of teaching you to accept, understand, and bring your feelings under *your* control, they will rely on commands, physical punishment, shame, or depriving you of affection and privileges to bring you in line. If that does not work, then they might try to double their commands and punishment or give up on you and try to hand the responsibility over to others. Unfortunately, later on when you are on your own, you will tend to treat your feelings the same way. You will try to crush them, give in to them, or give up on them. You might never understand where they fit into your life.

So at a critical time, others play a very important part in your life. They start you off. Although how you live and finish your life does not depend entirely on how you began it, the beginning is important. Without going overboard, you can rightly praise or blame others for the start they gave you.

Another Start

What can you do if you have not become an independent person? How do you handle the dos and don'ts of your training if they have been running your life? How do you handle your feelings if they have been in control of you?

Obviously, you cannot houseclean your brain and throw all the dos and don'ts of your training out the window. They might be the only control you have over your impulsive feelings. Nor can you simply knock on the locked doors of your feelings and tell them to open up. If they have been sealed under the lock and key of "I don't care," they are not going to open up easily.

As at the start of your life you needed others to help you become an independent person, you will probably need a similar kind of help to make a new start. You will need sensitive and independent people to show you how to listen to your training and your feelings and how to deal with them without letting them take control. Such helpers will need to be *capable* and *willing*. One without the other is no good.

Where will you find such people?

They are to be found. Every age and every society has a chosen group of people who have found themselves and have built their lives on reality. Having gone through the experience of becoming real, they are willing to share both their findings and themselves with you. All they ask of you is that you *honestly* want to find yourself and are *ready* and *willing* to do so.

On Your Part

So, whether you luckily have found people who can help you or your pain of loneliness, depression, and always being scared on the inside have forced you to look for help, you must do your part in becoming real. This will require making adjustments to the demands of your training and your feelings and being willing to *assert* your real personality by making your own decisions.

First, on the part of your training, you will have to stop excusing yourself or blaming others when you perform poorly. You are not perfect. If you have performed poorly, then you have performed poorly. All the erasers and all the mental anguish to convince yourself that you did not do poorly will not erase the facts. It is something you will have to accept.

Second, on the part of your feelings, you will have to take some chances. If you have convinced your feelings never to care about others again because you have been hurt too many times, you will have to take some baby steps toward caring about others. You are no longer a helpless child, and the persons you now want to trust and care about are mature enough not to take advantage of you. They are willing to "turn the other cheek" or "walk the extra mile" rather than pounce on you or put you down when you fail to live up to what is expected of you. On your part, even though you are ready to run back into yourself at the slightest sign of betrayal, you must be willing to take the first, fearful steps of coming out of yourself.

Third, having considered the dos and don'ts of your training and the wishes and desires of your feelings, you will have to decide what is best for you as a whole person. You should stay with your decision regardless of how much your training or feelings might object.

On the Part of Others

The first thing that others who are going to help you must do is to realize that no matter how capable you are of doing a lot of things, you are only a beginner when it comes to standing independently and tall on your own. You are so accustomed to leaning on your training or others or running off wildly after the whims of your impulsive, gluttonous, or sexual feelings that it will take a lot of good example, time, and effort not to do so. Until you see and are convinced of the benefits of being responsible to yourself, you will tend to fall back into old ways of doing things. It is hoped that it will not happen often and that it will not last for long.

So, the person helping you will need a good supply of patience as you sort out the dos and don'ts of your training, listen to your feelings, and then decide what to do. He or she will need extra patience when you slip back into old worries or irresponsible ways of acting.

Your helper must also be ready with a lot of encouragement. Your feelings need a great deal of encouragement to overcome the fear of trying new things or of trying old things in a new way. New experiences bring out new feelings, many of them scary. It takes determination to try a new hairstyle, make new friends, or try a new kind of work. It will help immensely if you have the reassurance of others while you are attempting these new things.

It will be of profit here to point out that others must avoid extremes in encouraging your efforts.

First, even your small gains should not go unnoticed. They should be praised. You should not have to wait until you have done something big before you are praised.

Second, the recognition that is given must be truthful. Small gains are only small gains — no more, no less. So you do not have to be misled or scared off by your gains because you fear that everyone thinks you are so much better than you are.

Joining Hands

In this consideration of you and your relationship with others, you can see how helpful other people can be. If you had to, you could become a real, independent person on your own. Others have done it. But how much easier and healthier it is to have others help you. Their help enables you to resist the temptation to ignore your training and everything that others have taught you. Their help also insures you that once you have become independent you will also be interdependent. You will not be a loner. Having tasted and shared a meaningful relationship with others, you will want to continue to do so.

Not to go out to others is to build *U-turn* roads. You never go very far from yourself. Eventually that has to hurt you.

To violate others' rights to life, possessions, and truth is worse. You not only compromise your real self by giving in to whims and impulses, you destroy others' trust in you. You have taken something from them that they could have shared with you.

So your growth as a healthy individual is best assured when you join your hands with other people.

It is further assured when one of those other persons is God. Other human beings can do much for you in becoming mature and independent, but he can do more. We will consider your relationship with God in our next and final chapter.

Questions

1. Is there someone you depend on too much? What benefits do you get from being so dependent? What does it cost you? Do you like having someone depend on you? Is that necessarily bad?
2. Do you know any independent people? What are they like?
3. How did they become independent people? What is their secret? Are they slaves either to their "image" or to their impulsive feelings?
4. To become an independent person, do you have to step on a lot of toes or not care what others think of you? What is the difference between being independent and being isolated?
5. Is it hard to become an independent person? Are there people in your life who would oppose

you? Would they rather that you stayed dependent? How can someone help you become independent?

6. Could you handle an interdependent relationship where the emphasis is more on want than on need?

8
WHEN
THE OTHER
IS GOD

In dealing with others, you have seen that your relationship should outgrow a need for them and become a want. You are independent of others, but you want them.

Your relationship with God should be like that. It should go from a child's "gimme" relationship to an adult, loving relationship. In some ways, your relationship with God will always be a need relationship. In other ways, it will not. We will consider your dependency on God first and then your independency.

A Dependent Relationship

In dealing with God, you can never outgrow the need for him.

As the intricate designs found in cars, television sets, and skyscrapers need an intelligent designer to explain how they came to be, natural things such as trees, animals, and people need an intelligent designer to explain how they have come to be. This is being realistic. It is not letting your imagination pretend that things just happen.

Who is this intelligent designer?

We call this designer "God." You exist because God created you and continues to create you from moment to moment. Your relationship or connection with God is many times greater than the umbilical cord relationship you had with your mother. After nine months you were able to leave your mother's womb and live. You can never leave God's sustaining power and continue to exist.

This is reality.

If you are not aware of this reality, then you are depriving yourself of your foundation in being. You are also depriving yourself of a contact with the one person who gives you being in an enduring way. Others can affect your being and well-being, but not like God.

While other human beings are the topsoil you need for developing your personality, God is the root soil. To have no contacts with God is like a tree whose deep roots are severed. It can still be nourished by the topsoil it is clinging to, but it is deprived of the deep support it needs. It does not amount to very much. It is this way with human beings who do not know or ignore God in their lives.

The Need for Revelation

So your need of God is basic.

Also your need for a knowledge of God is basic.

"But," you might object, "it is so hard to get to know God as he really is. Sure, nature shows us a lot about God, but that is not very personal. That is more clinical or scientific. That is like analyzing a person's handwriting and concluding what kind of person he is or was. If only God would speak to us and tell us about himself, we could really get to know him."

Fortunately, God has spoken to us in ways more personal than through what he has created. In a kind of official way he has revealed himself, not to everyone but to special people who would be trustworthy in passing his message on to others. Their dealings with God are recorded in the Scriptures or the Bible.

The heart of God's message about himself and the world he created is simple. He tells us that he is a God of goodness. There is no evil in him. If evil exists in the world, it is not from him. It is from another source. It comes from an exclusion of God or from a failure to use God's creation as he designed it. His design was not to make a perfect world. It is a good world, but it is not perfect. It is a world that needs working on. Often it is the presence of defects in the material world that tests and helps us develop our spiritual capacities and become a whole person.

This wholeness or integrity that we are to attain is the thread that begins in the first pages of the Old Testament and weaves itself throughout the Bible up to the last pages of the New Testament. God created us "whole" and with integrity. Unfortunately, we did not stay that way. In fact, we stumbled and fell so badly that God had to make a major adjustment; he sent his own Son, in the person of Jesus Christ, to heal us of our broken relationship with God.

Christ — A Model and More

So we have in Jesus Christ the image of the Father. In this way God is speaking and dealing with us in a most personal way. Christ is God's Word. "In the beginning was the Word; the Word was in God's presence, and the Word was God" (John 1:1). Listening to and understanding Christ, we are learning about God as he is.

We also have in the human aspects of Jesus Christ a perfect example of what it means to be a real person.

Christ has feelings, deep feelings, but he is more than his feelings.

Christ knows and respects his training, but he uses it to bring it to perfection, not to hinder his growth.

Christ has a human intellect that grew with wisdom, but he was not just an intellect.

Christ was a *whole* person. He could give himself back to his Father completely because he had his full self to give. That is the breathtaking marvel of the humanity of Christ.

But Christ was more than a whole person. He was and is also God.

So Christ is not just someone we follow. In a sense, he is someone we become.

"How is that possible?" you ask. "I thought that being a person means you never become someone other than yourself, your real self."

God's Plan

As there are many different degrees of light, there are many different degrees of sharing in God's life. In our material-spiritual creation, God wants us humans to have the highest sharing in his life. Our life is so much higher than that of plants or animals.

How much life does God share with us?

It depends. God has a plan for us that has two parts. The amount of his life that we share or experience depends on how well we fulfill both parts of his plan.

The first part of God's plan is what he gives us as our own, regardless of how we use it or fail to use it or even abuse it. This is ours, and God will never take it back or destroy it. It always remains there. It is our natural self, the whole self we have been considering. It is the self we can become and are most fully conscious of.

The second part of God's plan is an additional sharing in his life. It is a supernatural or above-natural sharing in God's personal life. It is almost the way the human part of Christ shares in the personal life of his Father. It is almost too wonderful to even hint at with words.

However, this higher sharing in God's life is conditional. It depends on how we develop or use the talents God has given us.

If we use them well, then God gives us this higher sharing in his personal life both now and hereafter. *Now* we only have a minimum awareness of what we are sharing. *Later* we will have a full awareness and delight.

If we do not use our talents well, then God will not give us this higher sharing in his personal life.

Incorporation

If we fulfill the conditions necessary for a sharing in God's personal life, that automatically unites us to Christ. Whether we are actually aware of it or not, we become one with him. As smaller businesses become incorporated in a bigger business, we become incorporated into Christ. In a strange but real way, we become one with Christ.

St. John describes this incorporation in terms of a vine and its branches. He records the words of Jesus himself: "I am the vine, you are the branches" (John 15:5).

St. Paul describes it in terms of a body. He says, "You, then, are the body of Christ. Every one of you is a member of it" (1 Corinthians 12:27).

Because of this becoming one with Christ, we have a whole new motive for our actions. Not only in dealing with others but also in dealing with ourselves, we take on a dignity vastly superior to that of our human nature. In a strange way we have become Christ. So, to do wrong to others or to ourselves would be to do wrong to Christ. "Do you not see that your bodies are members of Christ? Would you have me take Christ's members and make them the members of a prostitute?" (1 Corinthians 6:15) To help others and ourselves is to help Christ. "I assure you, as often as you did it for one of my least brothers, you did it for me" (Matthew 25:40). Or as St. Paul would put it, "Defer to one another out of reverence for Christ" (Ephesians 5:21).

So we are all invisibly united to Christ; and for those of us who have been privileged to be sacramentally baptized, we are also visibly united to him. Around and on St. Peter, the rock, we form his Church.

As you can see, this incorporation into Christ adds a whole new dimension to our lives. Imagine what this could mean to ourselves and others if this supernatural structure has our intact, real self as its basis. The often-used expression is that grace builds on nature. What a building, what a winning combination, it would be for grace or freely given supernatural life to have our whole, real self as its partner.

A Fuller Picture

So the real person God wants you to be includes both your natural life and the above-natural life that he wants to give you as a bonus.

In God's way of looking at these two lives, they are one and the same. As two lights in a room blend into one light, these two lives make one life. Although it is on a vastly lesser scale, they make your life very similar to the life of Jesus Christ. Becoming this special person, you become like another Christ. You have a perfect blending of a human and a higher life.

In our way of looking at these two lives, they are different. One is natural. The other is supernatural. One is deeply felt and experienced. The other is known to be there, even though it is not often felt.

Who are you supposed to be?

You are supposed to be a whole person whose life is a mingling of human life and a higher sharing in God's personal life.

An Independent Relationship

So, although you are very dependent on God, you are also independent of him. It is up to you to use your talents to become the person we have been describing. It is not all up to God. He has left a good part of your development in your hands.

This probably sounds so obvious, and yet many become confused and blame God when things go wrong. Instead of realizing that the *seemingly impossible* situation they are in is due to their lack of maturity and acceptance of reality, they look to God for a way out of it. They are not interested in learning from the experience and making adjustments inside of themselves. No, they have had it, and God *must* do something about it or they will lose confidence in him.

Assuredly, God does give extraordinary help in trying times, but he must do it in a way that will not interfere or harm your chances to grow and develop your own resources. God's way of safeguarding the part you must play is to insist on sustained prayer and effort on your part to better the situation. In this way you are doing *something*. You are not putting yourself in a totally dependent condition.

So it is important for you to become real and independent. God will help you. He will not do it for you.

A Belief in the Product

Although it might sound blasphemous to speak of being independent of God, it is not.

The truth is that it is high praise of God's workmanship.

It is saying, "God, you did a good job in making me. I am a remarkably well-put-together being who is capable of acting on the basis of the talent you have given me. I did not make me. You did, and you did a good job. To always come running to you and to expect you to give me special attention and help when I have not used what you have already given me is to act irresponsibly. So, God, I ask you to supervise the product I am making of my life, and I will call on you and others for special help when I need it, but I am going to try to work it out on my own. That does not mean that I am not going to be talking things over with you. No, it means that I believe in the gift of life you have given me. It is a good one. If I try to develop it to the best of my abilities, I am sure you will take care of what I cannot handle. You see, I not only believe in the product you have made, I also believe in you."

A Help

How can you explain these two needs that you have — a need for God and a need to act on your own?

Perhaps the illustration of a fish's relationship to water might help you see this a little better.

A fish absolutely needs a suitable amount of water to stay alive. It cannot do without it. And yet, being sustained by the water that surrounds it is not enough. The fish must do its part. It must seek out and obtain food to nourish and maintain itself.

You are in a similar condition. You absolutely need God to explain and sustain your being. Without him you cannot exist. And yet, you must do your part. You must take upon yourself the responsibility of your development.

When you have developed enough so that your real self is in control of you, not your training nor your impulsive feelings, then you can go to God as a free person.

It is not as a *carefree* person, but as a

responsible person who has respect for reality and relationships.

It is as a person eager to understand and abide by the workings of God's creation.

It is as a person eager to participate in the special plans God has added to creation by giving us Jesus Christ.

It is as a person eager to know and follow the truth about God, your real self, and others as best you can.

When you can go to God as this free person, you will see God in a new light. While God will always be Lord, he will also become Love. What happens then on the natural and supernatural levels of your being is intimate and personal to God and you. And it is only the beginning. As St. John exclaims, "Dearly beloved, we are God's children now; what we shall later be has not yet come to light. We know that when it comes to light we shall be like him, for we shall see him as he is" (1 John 3:2).

Questions

1. In what ways do you need God? How do you recognize or show this need?
2. Why do you need God to tell you about himself through Revelation?
3. What special plans in Christ does God have for you?
4. In what way are you independent of God? Would you still exist if you never acknowledged God or prayed to him?
5. Do you have a loving or a fearing relationship with God?

CONCLUSION

As you come to the last pages of this book, has *who you really are* become any clearer?

This knowledge of your true self is your only guarantee that you will be able to survive and profit from these unsettled times.

You can no longer let the dos and don'ts of your training replace you. Not only do many of those dos and don'ts belong to another time and culture and must be worked on before they can be of use now, but they cannot successfully take the place of your real self.

Nor will the 1,001 ways of having sex described and illustrated in magazines and books satisfy the empty spaces in your longings.

No, only a sincere search for yourself will do. You need the precautions and guidelines of your training. You need the vital power of your feelings, but only the strong force of your real personality can help you ride the rapids of these changing times.

So many are in search of an identity. They want and need something that remains the same, despite all the changes. As we have seen, that something should be your real self. It alone can have you standing tall and firm in these changing times.

But, even if the times were not so challenging, you would owe it to yourself and others to let the masterpiece of your real personality — human and elevated — shine through, so that you can be happy and God can be praised for making you the wonder that you are. God deserves it for investing so much of his love and caring in you. You deserve it in proportion to the efforts you are making to live your life to the full.

Who are you, really? We have considered who you can be. It is up to you to decide who you will be.

Questions

1. Having read this book, do you have a better self-image?
2. Are you more determined to be your real self?
3. Are you willing to praise God for one of his finest creations — yourself?